The Civilization of the American Indian Series

(*Complete list on page 88*)

TALES FROM THE MOHAVES

TALES
FROM THE
MOHAVES

✚ ✚ ✚ ✚ ✚

By HERMAN GREY

with a foreword
by Alice Marriott

UNIVERSITY OF OKLAHOMA PRESS : NORMAN

*The paper on which this book is printed bears the water-
mark of the University of Oklahoma Press and has an
effective life of at least three hundred years.*

INTERNATIONAL STANDARD BOOK NUMBER: 0–8061–0899–1

LIBRARY OF CONGRESS CATALOG CARD NUMBER: 69–16731

COPYRIGHT 1970 BY THE UNIVERSITY OF OKLAHOMA PRESS,
PUBLISHING DIVISION OF THE UNIVERSITY. COMPOSED AND
PRINTED AT NORMAN, OKLAHOMA, U.S.A., BY THE UNIVERSITY
OF OKLAHOMA PRESS. FIRST EDITION.

82049

FOREWORD

by
Alice Marriott

Readers are seldom privileged to have an opportunity as rare as the one this book affords them. Seldom, indeed, are the great myths of a people written by one of the people themselves. Here we have such a book, and reading it is a delight.

Mr. Grey is a Mohave. He is Shul-ya, of the Beaver Clan. He writes as a Mohave, but in the literate English of today. He has written these myths and legends primarily for his children, so that their teacher may read them—and how one envies teacher and classmates the listening!

Some intensive studies of Mohave life were made by graduates of the University of California in the late 1920's and early 1930's. One thinks of Leslie Spier's

Yuman Tribes of the Gila River, of Darryl Ford's *Havasupai Ethnography*, and above all of Alfred Kroeber's tremendous compendium, *Handbook of the Indian Tribes of California*, which includes the Mohaves, and of Frances Densmore's studies of Mohave and Yuman music. Ruth Underhill, who did intensive work along the Gila and Colorado rivers, still confined her published work to the Pimas and Papagos.

In the forties, fifties, and sixties, anthropologists turned their collective attention farther afield, to Asia, Africa, and Oceania. Since then, the American Indian has stood as the professionally forgotten man.

Indeed, the only book that sticks in the mind as giving a *feeling* of Mohave life, as well as the bare bones of fact, is Charles McNichols' *Crazy Weather*—not an ethnographic study at all, but a novel. It is, as a matter of fact, a sort of southwestern *Huckleberry Finn*, and rereading it after reading Mr. Grey's stories gives one almost a sensation of *déjà vu* as one realizes how deeply boyhood experiences with this most remarkable people can sink into the adult unconsciousness. The two books really should be read together.

These myths are left as Mr. Grey wrote them in his own language. They are a remarkable addition not only to the field of general North American anthropology but also to the specific field of American Indian mythology.

An anthropologist, as he works in the field, is always one jump ahead of the undertaker. He snatches and he grabs, lest invaluable information be gone before he can record it. Mr. Grey, working for his children in the timelessness that is the Mohave world, has not felt this drive. Hence the grace, the turn of phrase, the world that never was but should have been that his stories evoke.

Truly it is his awareness of his own people, combined with an unusual ability to objectify them, that gives Mr. Grey's book its greatest value. How many literate Indians, if asked, could produce such a statement as: "Conscious learning seems to him [the Mohave] nearly impossible, and he is convinced that he has dreamed for the first time, or has dreamed repetitiously, the things all Mohaves know in common."

On the other hand, the statement Mr. Grey makes that "it is impossible to tell through the words of another culture and another language the meaning of a Mohave dream. To do so would be to explain the nature of Faith—the indefinable" is all too familiar to Indians and anthropologists alike. It is the very fact that the intangibles cannot be recorded by an outsider that supplies the great value and substance of this book.

Reading it has been a pleasure. Being asked to write its foreword has been an honor. And to know that such a book exists is a privilege to an anthropologist and folklorist.

ALICE MARRIOTT

Oklahoma City, Oklahoma
September 1, 1970

PREFACE

The Mohave clings to his belief in dreams as a basis for everyday life. Not only all shamanistic power, but all myths, songs, bravery, fortune in battle, and good fortune in gambling derive from dreams. Every special event is dreamed. Knowledge is not a thing to be learned, a Mohave will say, but something to be acquired by each person through his dreaming.

All shamans say that they received their power from Mastamho, when he was put here on this earth. So deep are these convictions that, when old age comes, a Mohave can seldom distinguish between the dreams he has been told by an uncle or brother and what he has himself experienced. The Mohave learns as much from other people as from his own experience. Conscious learning seems to him nearly impossible, and he is convinced he has dreamed for the first time, or has dreamed repetitiously, the things which all Mohaves know in common. It is a strange attitude to us, and one that could only have grown out of this remarkable Indian culture.

There is, too, an amazing timelessness in Mohave belief and awareness, which finds its reflection in every song and myth of Mohave belief. The precise time of day or night will be specified for each supernatural event, but the briefest telling suffices for the growth from boyhood to adulthood, for the transformation from a person to an animal, or for the making of a mountain.

A man may give his song or story to his son or to some other close relative when he feels himself near to death or concludes that the person in question wishes to learn the story or song. Only one man may sing or tell a sequence of songs and stories, and thus the myths are inherited within the family and clan. A storyteller begins from a timeless source, with the statement that the story came to him from his uncle or brother and now belongs to him.

Dreams, then, are the foundation of Mohave life. Dreams are always stated as if they had been cast in mythological molds. In no other tribes are activities so controlled by this psychic state. In no other Indian culture is daily life so completely reflected in myths and songs.

Like other Indian groups, the Mohaves embody a hero in each myth. Little has been written about the mythological heroes Red Hand and Swift Lance. Many tribes have borrowed Mohave songs and myths, for the Mohaves were great travelers. They went as far as the northern California lake and hill tribes: the Wiyots, Hupas, Pomos, Shastas, Yokuts, and the Chumashes. The Mohaves visited southern California tribes as well: the Serranos, Gabrielinos, Luiseños, and Diegueños, all of them more familiarly known as Mission Indians. In a smaller radius the Mohaves traveled to the Hopis, Walapais, Maricopas, Pimas, and Papagos. Often the Mohaves allied themselves with the Western Apaches to raid the Pimas and Papagos.

The character of Swift Lance was originally dreamed by a person who has now passed from this world, and so his name cannot be spoken. I have told his stories here for his children and grandchildren, and for my own children and their children.

HERMAN GREY

Scottsdale, Arizona
September 1, 1970

CONTENTS

	Foreword, by Alice Marriott	*page vii*
	Preface	*xi*
	Introduction	3
1	Swift Lance	17
2	The Mohave Nation	25
3	The Frog People	33
4	The Fire Ghost	47
5	Coyoteman	55
6	The Spirit Deer	61
7	The Courtship of Swift Lance	67
8	The Fate of Moonbeam	79
	Bibliography	87
	Map: Northern Mohave Reservation	7

TALES FROM THE MOHAVES

INTRODUCTION

The "Dreamings" and the legends derived from them have always represented the culture and the unity of the Mohave people. Now the Dreamings are slowly dying out and are being lost. The facts and myths on which they are based have been handed down within the family and clan.

The "Sings" and the "Great Tellings" on which Dreamings are based belong to the older people. As younger people leave the reservation to obtain jobs, marry into other tribes, and begin new lives, the old tribal customs weaken and are forgotten. The once-typical Mohave traits and interests merge with those of other cultures.

The history of the Mohaves is fairly well known and

is available in other books. I will summarize it here, in the belief that a general knowledge of Mohave characteristics will enable readers better to understand the secrets that hve always distinguished the Mohaves.

The home range of the Mohaves—the most northerly of the Yuman-speaking tribes—centered in the lower Colorado River valley. Some of the Yuman speakers were hereditary enemies of the Mohaves, especially the Halchidhomas, the Maricopas, and the Cocopas, while the Yumas proper and the Mohaves have always been allies.

It was an extensive area, including the Mohave Valley, which lies within the present states of Arizona, California, and Nevada. Soil and climate proved suitable for farming and sheep raising, after the introduction of European methods of agriculture and domesticated animals. Land was privately owned and was inherited through the male line. Men did most of the field work.

Each family had its designated plot of land, marked by boundary stakes which were painted or feathered. The early dwellings were open-sided, flat-roofed shades. Poles supported the arrowweed thatch of the roof, and the spaces between the poles were used for storage. These were the summer houses. In winter rectangular houses were built, with sloping sides of poles interlaced with arrowweed stalks and daubed with earth. A still later house type was a gabled structure.

Mohave men wore breechclouts of woven inner willow bark. The women wore knee-length aprons, front and back, made of the same material. Woven rabbit-skin blankets were worn by both sexes in cold weather. Plaited sandals were worn when the people went traveling.

Physically, Mohave men were tall, thin, and muscular. The women were shorter and were inclined to be stout. Skin coloring was light brown with a slight yellow tone. The women wore their hair long in back, with bangs over their foreheads. The men twisted their hair into numerous thin strands. Both men and women were proud of having long black hair and frequently washed it in a combination of slough mud, mashed mesquite-bark gum, and water. The compound was plastered over the hair and allowed to remain for days. Soap was also obtained from pounded yucca or agave roots.

Tattooing was common. Usually red paint was preferred, but sometimes white paint was applied to the body. The ear lobes were pierced for the suspension of strings of white shell beads. Young men also pierced the nasal septum and inserted horizontal bone slivers or shell ornaments.

Arts and crafts were few. The women made some

pottery by the paddle-and-anvil method, painted it with cottonwood, turtle, or rattlesnake designs, and fired it a reddish-buff tone. Both the pottery and the coiled basketry the women stitched were for household use, not for sale or decoration, and therefore were stronger and more durable than decorative.

Although Mohave life followed the river courses, the people did not use canoes. Instead, when a stream was too high or strong to wade or swim across, the men made rafts by binding together bundles of cattails.

Maize, beans, squash, pumpkins, and gourds were cultivated with sharpened digging sticks or with flattened, hoelike wooden paddles. The use of the deer-scapula hoe, common among the Hopis and the Río Grande farmers, was apparently not known to the Mohaves. Field irrigation depended on river flooding, and crops were planted when the water had gone down. This method is known as "bola," or "pocket," irrigation.

The Mohaves were a warlike people. Raiding and going on war parties were a favorite outdoor sport, one which reached a degree of professionalism that might be referred to as an occupation. Torture of prisoners was uncommon; when a fight was over, it was ended. There was great fear of the return of the dead, and men who had killed enemies in battle went

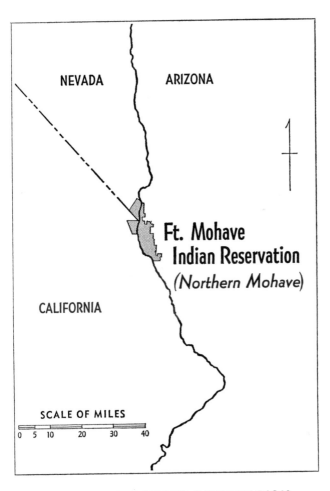

NORTHERN MOHAVE RESERVATION

through an elaborate cleansing ritual before they rejoined their families.

War bows were large, often as tall as the men who drew them. The staves were of screw-bean, willow, or mesquite trunks, scraped down with pieces of shell or volcanic glass, heated, and bent into shape. Sinew or other backing was not used on these bows. Deer-sinew strings were used. The arrows were sharpened stalks of arrowweed, with three-feather vaning. No tips were used; the stalks were sharp enough to pierce a man or a deer.

Probably the most characteristic Mohave weapons were the war clubs. They ranged from straight screw-bean sticks, through malletlike clubs of ironwood or mesquite, to the famous "potato mashers," short-handled clubs which were carried only by the bravest men. Circular deer-hide shields were carried in hand-to-hand fighting.

The Mohaves were extensive traders. They traveled north to the Yumas and went south to exchange rabbit-skin blankets, paint, baskets, and other articles with the Shoshoni tribes. A test of endurance for men was a trip into southern California, the whole distance covered at a jogging trot, to trade for abalone shells. The Mohaves went as far afield as the Yokuts of the San Joaquin area.

Like other Yuman peoples, the Mohaves had exogamous clans which descended in the male line. Names denoting clan affiliation were given only to women. Marriage within the clan was forbidden, and each clan had its own chief (the *kohata*).

Clan names, derived from natural phenomena, were as follows:

Nyo-ilcha	Sun
Hoalya	Moon
Mat-hatchva	Wind
Owich	Cloud
Hipa (or Huk-thar)	Coyote
Moha	Mountain Sheep
Shul-ya	Beaver
Masipa	Quail
Vahadha	Tobacco
Mothaho	Screech Owl

Mohave religion was informal, without personal-ized gods or ritual dances. There were remote beings, whose legendary deeds explained the origin of the Mohaves. Their leading spirit, Matavilya, was the firstborn of the union of Sky and Earth. Matavilya was killed by his daughter, Frog Woman, and in turn was succeeded by his son, Mastamho. Mastamho taught the Mohaves their way of life. His climaxing deed on earth was to kill the sea monster, Sky Rattle-snake. With his tasks accomplished, Mastamho quickly turned himself into an eagle and flew away.

Without deities, and now without a culture hero, legends became the symbols and sources of power to the Mohaves. An individual reached the supernaturals through the "Great Dreams."

Shamans, in particular, relied on dreaming for guidance. One could cure disease caused by sorcerers or ghosts by laying on of hands, singing, or blowing a spray of saliva over the patient. A shaman could also cause disease, but only at the risk of being killed by the vengeful relatives of his victims.

Dreaming was the very core of Mohave life. It was the source of each individual's special skill, of his prowess as a warrior, and of his success in all his undertakings. A Great Dream might foretell the birth of a male child to his father. Later the dream would return to the child as he grew to manhood and listened to others tell of their dreams. Then he dreamed his own and became a man.

A Mohave believed that in his dreams he went back to the source of creation. The origin of all things was revealed to him. The life of the Spirit World appeared before his eyes, to be seen as through a veil.

It is impossible to tell through the words of another culture and another language the meaning of a Mohave dream. To do so would be to explain the nature of faith—the indefinable. It is the same with the quality of Mohave dreams. They are very real; they exert tremendous power on everything an individual thinks or does. They are still potent forces in Mohave life, although the outward expression of dreams through Sings and Great Tellings has greatly diminished, and with it the closeness and unity of Mohave life.

Great Dreams were sung or told to audiences. If the formalized telling did not conform to traditional ways, elders were present to correct the teller. Dream Telling was intended to illuminate the future and to bring help, hope, and encouragement to each listener as he applied his own interpretation to what he heard. In the Dream Telling, each listener found symbols and meanings which were his alone.

The Great Tellings (Ich-kamava) and Sings related legends of persons, places, and happenings. Often they were based on historical events, or the events were incorporated in the telling. Tellings were not religious in nature, and no special masks or clothing, except perhaps a skullcap of owl feathers, was worn. Faces and bodies of the singers were often painted before the telling began.

The musical accompaniment of a Sing was the humming of gourd rattles small enough to be carried in a man's pockets and the sound of drumming on an overturned basket. The Sing might last through one or several nights and the intervening days.

There were thirty Sing cycles, some of which can be listed as follows:

Yellaka	Goose
Akaka	Raven
Itacha	Pleiades
Oth-i	Salt
Akwaka	Deer
Kapata	Turtle

Few people are with us now who can remember the names of all thirty cycles, or repeat the 150 to 200 songs of each cycle.

When the Mohaves drove the Halchidhomas out of their lands, the Chemehueyis tried to move into the Mohave Valley. The Mohaves drove the Chemehuevis back into the desert, but in the process divided into the Northern and Southern Mohave groups. In time each division developed its own legends, but always within the pattern of the cycle of thirty.

So deep is the belief in dreams, and the legends with which they are interwoven, that no Mohave sings one without enumerating exact details and locations. Sometimes new details are extemporized by the teller. The songs tell of war, bravery, myths, history, heroes, travel, places, or curing. In the old days, singers also had their own songs. Sometimes these songs were handed down to younger relatives and so have survived, but others were lost when the singers died.

During a Sing, a singer might stop at a certain interval. He would be asked to repeat the songs, to continue, or to allow another man to take up the same series. As he learned and studied the songs, a singer gained further insight into their meanings. These could be added to the song.

A dream might be an actual nocturnal one, or it might be a continued thought or a flash of insight which gave a further comprehension and contemplation of the man's hopes and perceptions. Dreams might give foresight of some obstacle to the achievement of an end and might also reveal the means of overcoming the obstruction. Many times a dream foretold a coming event, such as the outcome of a raid or the fate of a warrior.

A Sing might honor an event, such as the coming of age of a daughter. At such times there was always plenty of food, and the Sing might continue for a long time. A family might celebrate such an occasion as a private affair, or it might be an occasion in which the whole clan participated.

Dreams were the natural and logical expression of Mohave philosophy. They were not peyote-induced hallucinations or the result of a conscious vision-quest. Dreams came to give wisdom and insight. The intense concentration of the group of listeners and the feeling of companionship their presence engendered were a part of the spell of the Telling.

All this force unfortunately must be lost in translation. Mohave words, like those of any language, have their own subtleties and secret undertones that can never be interpreted. They lose flavor in literal translation.

People of other races find it hard to grasp the Mohave belief that knowledge comes only partly through experience. In each man it is enhanced by his dreams. Mohave people have the ability to adapt to other ways and to acquire the skills of persons with whom they work and are in association. But Mohave solidarity is unique. The people are joined to one another by the invisible bonds of an ancient cultural heritage. Psychic feelings guide Mohave activities as dream cycles guide the course of life's behavior.

I am a Mohave. These tales were told to me by an uncle who has left us now.

One dark, stormy night, when I was very young, we were crossing the Colorado on our way home to Fort Mohave on the Arizona side of the river. I was handling the oars, and my uncle was poling. Suddenly he slipped and fell into the water. He was a husky man and, like all Mohaves, an excellent swimmer, so he got back to the boat readily.

We beached the boat. During the two-mile walk home, my uncle began to sing a song that I had never heard before. Late that night, as we sat beside the fire, he told me a story he had learned in a series of dreams.

Later I heard a similar tale from a Yuma Indian, who may have dreamed it or may have heard it from my uncle at a Sing. I know that the trip to Apacheland and the battles with the Pimas are factual. The rest of the tale is legend.

So I have written these tales as I learned them. Originally I put them together for my own children, who wanted to take them to school for their teacher to read. That was the beginning. Since then I have studied further and expanded the tales.

I am a Mohave. I am Shul-ya, of the Beaver Clan.

SWIFT LANCE

The winter had been long and hard, but now the sun sent a little more heat with its increased rays. The sharp breeze that came in from the river lost some of its stinging bite. The north mountain faces were less cold, almost smiling. A new world with its tiny green buds was pushing its way into spring.

"Hear, all people, hear the good news! A Mohave is born this day!"

Every dwelling sent forth people to learn of the great event.

"Falling Leaves presents a man-child this day to Long Lance!"

The people gathered about the dwelling of Long Lance to share in the presentation.

From the hands of Falling Leaves, Long Lance accepted his son. His strong fingers pressed firmly around the tiny chest, thrilling to the beating of the vigorous young heart. He held the boy facing the east and, addressing the Source of All Life, spoke his prayer:

> Mighty Sun, giver of life,
> As thou dost rise from the east,
> Wilt thou pause in thine upward way
> To look upon our home this day,
> Giving him promise of a good
>   and useful life.

To the north Long Lance turned, still holding the boy aloft:

> North winds, source of all swiftness,
> Wilt thou pause in the blowing
> To breathe fleetness
> Into the body of my son this day,
> That he may go his way with light feet,
> Reaching far places with thine own ease.

Turning to face the west, he continued:

> High clouds of the west, givers of wisdom,
> Favor my son this day
> And throughout all his days,
> That he may know
> The way he should travel,

And walk straight in the paths
That lead to his greater self.

To the south he spoke:

Home of the storms, givers of strength,
Teach my son to bend
Before the wild force of the winds;
To pause, and gather his forces
For what lies ahead
When it is time to walk before thy fury,
To go on his way in calm certainty
When thy turbulence shall subside.

Thus was the son of Long Lance welcomed into
the life of the village, and so was he prepared to begin
his earth life. No name was he given. A nickname
would serve his first year, then he would be given a
name to use until he earned one for himself.

His first ten years would be free of all restraint. He
would roam the desert, swim in the river, fish as the
whims of youth might lead his group of playmates—
without chores to be done or a time schedule to be
met. Carefree as the animals that grew with them,
the boys would learn to be at home wherever they
found themselves, to make do with what Nature
provided, to choose friends.

So the son of Long Lance grew straight as an arrow,
swift as the wind. He listened carefully when Long

Lance told him the legends of their people, stories of ghosts and battles, tales of Nature and of other tribes. Together they sang the songs of the Mohaves; the songs of the bird, the bear, the turtle, and the river; and the songs of war.

Then one morning Long Lance led his son into the hills, carrying a single water gourd. His days of play were over; the time had come for his first lesson in obedience.

"My son, you will stay in these hills alone for the next three days. So long as your gourd supplies you, you may drink water, but for three days and three nights no food shall pass your lips. You will observe the animals and the growing things about you and think of the generosity of the Great Father who watches over all and gives to us what we must have to maintain life. When you return to your people, you will have chosen a name by which you will be known henceforth forever. Then shall your training begin, that you may earn the right to wear that name proudly."

Then was the boy alone with Nature and her children.

He lay for a time watching a colony of ants moving through the grasses, and he wondered that such tiny beings should be so knowing as they went about their work. He swallowed a mouthful of his precious water and turned on his back to see a flock of birds flying in a pattern against the sky. He slept, and when he awoke the first sunset fires were coloring the west. One last bird crossed the brilliance like a lance thrown swiftly by a strong arm. He smiled, settled more comfortably against the ground, and waited for the night to come.

The second day was filled with many things. He was restless and eager to find the message the Great Father had written on the face of the earth for him to read. Every tree that rose above him, every leaf that brushed his cheek, every stirring thing whispered to him; but strain as he would, his ear could not catch their meanings. When he returned to his resting place, it was again the time of sunset.

He tipped the gourd, and as the last swallow of water trickled down his throat, he smiled. Again that late bird made its swift and lancelike flight across the coral and gold of the sun's departure.

That night his dreams were laced together by the flight of a bird across a vivid sky; and when his eyes opened to behold a bird watching him thoughtfully from a nearby branch, he could think of nothing else. Surely this bird was an omen. The hunger pangs of his empty belly were as nothing. The dryness of his throat was a blessing if it brought him wisdom to understand what he saw.

When Long Lance came for his son, he found the boy sitting cross-legged, his back against a tree, gazing upward at the branch where the bird no longer sat.

"Have you found your name, my son?"

The boy stood tall, and his eyes were bright. "I am Swift Lance, son of Long Lance, whose father was Fire Lance, the warrior. In the quiet of this lonely spot I have learned many things. Now let us return to our dwelling, that I may listen to your teachings and become a man among men in the footsteps of my father."

Then did Long Lance rest his arm about the shoulders of his son, and in quiet pride he spoke.

"All that I have learned from the elders will I share with you, my son. You will learn all that I know, and more, for you must go further than I.

"We will hunt first, tracking the desert creatures to their lairs. You will practice the fighting ways with your friends, under the guidance of our bravest warriors, and when you are well trained, you will go with the braves into battle. The secrets of planting and growing things, the best ways of harvesting the food crops and storing them for the long cold winter, the knowledge of herbs and the making of medicines— all these a man must know to provide for and protect his family.

"Swift Lance will go far, but for now it is enough

that we return to our dwelling and partake of the food your mother has prepared with a prayer in her heart for your well-being."

So it was that a boy was born and nurtured and found his name and lived to make Swift Lance a hero to his people, the Mohaves.

THE MOHAVE NATION

Early one morning, as the sun sent its golden rays over the dark-gray mountains, bringing life to all they touched, the rays seemed to seek out the dark corners of the dwellings in Swift Lance's village. Swift Lance came out from his dwelling, stretching his arms wide and throwing back his head as he greeted the sun's rays that pierced his body, sending warmth all over him.

"Ho!" Swift Lance said. "This is the day Grandmother will tell me the history of our people. This is the best time of the day for Grandmother, for the warmth of the sun gives her a clear mind, and she can better think of young days."

Swift Lance ran to her dwelling, coming to her as

she sat upon a buckskin on the ground. Swift Lance, stopping, watched the golden rays play upon the old woman's wrinkled face. Then he called softly, "Grandmother, will you tell me the history of our people?"

"A-yeah! Grandson, I knew it was you. I heard you coming before you saw me. Come sit by me as I take of the Giver of Life, and I will tell you the history of our people.

"In the Peninsula of Yucatán where the world began, the Great Creator left his people with the promise that he would come again. Choosing well, he left with certain men the knowledge of growing things: how to plant and raise good corn and wheat, beans and pumpkins, cotton, squash, and melons. With other men he left knowledge of the body, of healing and protective medicine, but he appointed no chief, for the time was not yet ripe.

"Without strong leaders, the people quarreled among themselves and wasted their strength in harmful practices. The Creator saw that their acts spoiled the earth, and he sent great floods to cleanse its surface, sparing only four families who lived most nearly as he had taught his people to live.

"The eldest of each family became that family's leader, and his word was heard with respect. Each leader was given two helpers, a wise one to guide the people in the planting of their crops and the hunting of animal food and a medicine man to keep body and soul one, in sickness and in health.

"Under the guidance of the twelve chosen ones, the people multiplied and prospered. All spoke the same tongue, each understanding his brother's words, and they worked together preparing for the time when they would be led to the land promised them long ago; though they knew not where or how they would find the way. The women made moccasins for the long journey, and meat was dried and packed, ready for travel.

"Then came *akaka*, the Raven Bird. Large as the largest dove was the Raven Bird that came among the people, flying from one group to another, pausing and waiting, then moving on.

"At last one tribesman spoke: "Have you seen this bird that is with us these days? He sits first on one branch and then on another, watching and waiting. Does he seem to you to have something to say? Think you the bird may be a messenger from the Great Creator?"

Owich, one of the leaders, looked up at the bird. Many thoughts were exchanged as the people stood together talking about the newcomer. After many had spoken, the leader of the family held up his hands for attention. There was a deep silence as all leaned forward to hear what he might say.

" 'In the days before the days our people recall, the Great Creator spoke of a land of promise prepared for his chosen ones. After the flooding waters found their place and the land was clear, he spoke again to our forefathers of the land to which the faithful should one day be led. A third time Man-Who-Does-Not-Touch-the-Ground told of the land to the north and said that there would come one to lead those who would follow to that far country.

" 'Many years have we waited. Three times the promise has been spoken. The bird may well be the messenger we await. We cannot know until we prepare to follow where the bird may lead. Are you willing to pack your belongings for a trip that may last no man knows how long, to a country no man has ever seen?'

"The silence held for a moment or two as the people thought of what such a journey might mean. Then hands were raised, and voices expressed confidence in their leader, in the bird, and in the Great Creator. They would go.

" 'It shall be so,' Owich spoke again. 'Let each of us return to his home and prepare his family for the long trip. When the sun rises tomorrow, if the bird still waits on yonder tree, we will follow where he leads.'

"As the family began their preparations for the journey, neighbors sensed that something strange was happening. Soon other family groups were coming together to study the bird and to wonder.

"So it was that the whole tribe watched the departure of the first clan. Each thought in his heart that he would see what came of this; it might be well to follow in their footsteps one day.

"As the family leader approached the tree where the bird waited on that morning, the bird rose high in the air and turned northward, sinking to a treetop near the horizon. There he waited throughout the day, and thus the pattern of their traveling was established.

"From near tree to far tree flew the bird, always taking care to stay where he could be seen and waiting until the clan came near before moving on. It took them from the rising to the setting of the sun to cover each part of the trail the bird marked for them. As the last of the family looked back, they could see the first of the next family following, and they smiled, for it was good to know that friends came to be with them in the new land.

"So at last they came to the mountains now called San Francisco Peaks, and there at the foot of the mountains they awaited the coming of those who followed. The bird had led them where wild fruits and nuts, seeds and food plants and game were plentiful to meet their needs.

"The day came when groups from the four families sat down together in a council of thanksgiving in the San Francisco foothills. The Cocopa family decided to settle along the lower Colorado River, and the Maricopa family moved east into the desert and came upon the Gila River, where they made their home.

"But the first clan to follow the bird saw that he was not yet ready to nest, and they continued in his wake. A summer and a winter had passed since they had left the Yucatán; as they traveled there had been births and deaths, joys and sorrows.

"One early spring day they found themselves in the Great Valley of the Colorado River. The spreading plains welcomed them. The 'goodwill bird' circled over them in farewell and in ever-widening circles soared into the distant blue, leaving them to build homes, to plant crops, to hunt, and to fish. They rejoiced, for they had found their long-promised home.

"As the people prospered and grew strong, they were called the Mohaves or the Wamakavas by their neighbors. From the main village on the east bank of the middle Colorado, the land of the Mohaves stretched west to the big salty blue water, east to the Río Grande villages, south to the Pima country, and to the northland of the Utes. The Mohaves ranged their widespread domain, on occasion allying with the Apaches to raid other tribes or to make war. Of all tribes, only the Mohaves did not fear the Apaches."

"It is a good story," Swift Lance said to his grandmother. "Is it true? Who told you of these things?"

"Ah, Swift Lance, you alone ask of these stories. You, who are a young leader, you must know all that we the old ones know. Yes, Grandson, the tale of the Mohave Nation is true. You see, there are the chosen ones among all the tribes who are the Keepers of these *Ich-ḳamava*, or Great Tellings. We, the chosen ones, are of the Singer Clans, for many of our stories are told in song, and we are taught when very young. We visit all the singers and people of Great Tellings, and we in turn teach others of our clan. Many times we have visitors from the Walapais, Cocopas, Yumas, and other tribes far toward the great blue salty waters, to learn our songs and tales. Wherever you travel among these tribes, you will hear of White Flower, your grandmother, for I am one of the last among the tribes who knows the Great Tellings."

THE FROG PEOPLE

When he was a little boy, Swift Lance often stood looking toward the tall north peaks. Wild and rough, they beckoned, urging Swift Lance to come nearer. Many times a day he looked in their direction, and each time their call came to him more clearly. When he was old enough, he asked his father how they were called.

"We Mohaves speak of them as the Forbidden Mountains, my son. Many men have gone into them; few have returned. It is well to walk far from their foothills."

His mother would not answer his questions. Though he saw the fear in her eyes, still Swift Lance felt he must know of the mountains. And so one day he walked to the dwelling of his grandmother, who knew many things and told them well.

She was weaving a basket beside the doorway of her dwelling. Swift Lance sat quietly beside her, awaiting her greeting. When he spoke her name, White Flower continued to weave the light and dark strands in the pattern of her choosing. She did not look up, but her quiet voice was welcoming.

"What is your wish, Son of my son?" she asked.

"I come to White Flower, mother of my father, she who knows many things. I have come to learn why the far north peaks are called the Forbidden Mountains."

"A boy's questions sometimes lead into trouble. Why do you ask about forbidden things, Swift Lance?" One glance she gave him as her fingers flew at their weaving.

"The dawn light on those northern slopes cries out to me, White Flower, and the twilight shadows creeping up their foothills remind me that another day has passed and still I have not come to them."

There was a quiet time while their eyes watched the strands move in and out as the pattern of the basket took shape. The old woman's voice was soft, as if her thoughts were far away, when she spoke again.

"Just so my father felt about those canyons to the north. Until that day the hunt led him too close."

Swift Lance moved nearer. He wanted every word to fall clearly upon his hungry ears. His heart beat faster as he leaned forward, his eyes now upon his grandmother's face.

"The ancient ones spoke of the evil creatures who dwelt there in the north mountains. Strange beings, better left alone; but I never knew a man whose eyes had seen the people of danger.

"I remember my father, Tall Warrior, staggering into the door of our dwelling more dead than alive, that day so long ago. As he searched for mountain sheep for the stewing kettles, he had followed their signs deeper into the foothills than the others of the hunting party. As he dropped to his knee beside a huge rock to look more closely at the track he followed, a damp and smelly creature dropped down upon him, and they struggled fiercely.

"Tall Warrior could not tell us these things. He could not speak of that dreadful clammy thing, when awake. Only in the night an evil dream would come upon him, and he would fight the enemy again. Then would he cry out in his sleep and sweat with the effort of the struggle until he drove away his attacker and fell unconscious there in a forbidden canyon. We came to know, in this way, what had happened.

"I know nothing more of those northern mountains, Swift Lance. I have been content to stay far from them with my people. You would do well to turn your back on their evil beauty that would lure you into danger, my grandson."

"I am grateful, Grandmother, for this story. I will keep it in my heart." As Swift Lance joined his friends in a race, he glanced back; White Flower's fingers still worked to form the basket that would hold much grain at harvest time.

The years passed. They taught Swift Lance wisdom and kindness that won the love of his people. Of all the runners he was the swiftest. When the young men wrestled to test their strength and skill, Swift Lance triumphed most often. He visited and traded with many tribes, walking in far places. Always the Forbidden Mountains stood where earth meets sky, waiting for him to come to them. Often he asked strangers what they knew of the north hills. None of them would answer. Dropping their eyes to the ground, the strangers would walk around him as though he were but a rock in the path.

Finally he made a plan. He could wait no longer to know for himself the mystery of the tall north peaks. He sought out his closest friend.

"Shy Owl, will you travel two days to the west with me, that we may hunt sheep in the mountains there?"

"Do we start upon our hunt this day or wait another sun's rising?"

After two days' hunting, Swift Lance suggested, "The sheep have gone from these hills and valleys, Shy Owl. Let us pursue them to the north mountains, that we may find meat for our people—unless you fear to approach the Forbidden Ones."

Shy Owl looked up from the sandals he had just mended. "You are the leader of this hunting party, Swift Lance. Where you lead, I will follow."

Swift Lance headed north at a brisk trot, closely followed by Shy Owl. A small pebble kept each boy's mouth moist and saved breath that might have been wasted in talk. Their thoughts raced ahead of them to the Forbidden Mountains, and just as the sun hid behind the highest peak, they reached the foothills.

"Let us camp here. This huge boulder will shelter us."

"It is good. I will start the fire while Swift Lance hunts our meat." Shy Owl's eyes were choosing tiny dead twigs even as he spoke. Not many minutes later the sweet smell of roasting jackrabbit promised comfort to their empty bellies. They fed well and were soon ready for rest.

"I will watch first," Shy Owl spoke. "When sleep threatens me, I will waken you for your watch."

Swift Lance rolled himself in his blanket and slept, almost before his reply had died on the night air. Soundly he slept until a feeling of unease came over him. His nostrils breathed the dank smell of stale water. He stirred, waking suddenly as slimy, damp arms like thongs encircled his neck; but even as he moved, two powerful, clammy legs clamped about his waist.

"Shy Owl!" he cried, before a crashing blow knocked his head back to the ground and wrapped him in grim darkness.

Water lapped at his face when Swift Lance regained consciousness. He opened his eyes but saw only haze. He tried to move, but his arms were bound to his body, and his body was trussed to a log on which he was being pulled through the water by a huge creature. His eyes followed the vine rope that bound him to the log, then connected him to the waist of the creature.

He closed his eyes, squeezing them tightly. Surely he dreamed! He opened them again. The big frog still walked before him on its hind legs, pulling the log easily.

As he stared, the frog creature turned, saw that he was awake, and croaked in a deep voice. Swift Lance saw that his captor was about as tall as a buck deer and almost as wide. It certainly was a frog! The ugly face with its bulging eyes studied him as it might have looked at a fly; it had a cavernous mouth and flaring nostrils.

Swift Lance did not notice the second frog monster

until the leader looked past him and spoke to his companion. Amazement grew as the young man recognized the Mohave tongue. Answers came from another pair of the creatures, who pulled a second log bearing Shy Owl. His friend still slept.

Other frog people swam with them. As they neared the shore, many other frog men came toward them with their curious gait, half-running, half-jumping. The Mohave croaking filled the air. Mother frogs, wearing bark aprons, carried large waterproof baskets filled almost to the top with water. On the surface of the pool many tadpoles swam about. This was indeed another world!

On shore the captors stood both logs on end. The hands of Swift Lance were tied behind his back. A rope was tied about his neck, holding him upright against the log, and hobbles were tied to his ankles. He watched them treating Shy Owl the same way, but Shy Owl's legs gave way and he fell down. His arms and legs were so still that he could scarcely move, but the creatures jerked him to his feet again.

A path opened through the crowd of strange beings. Straight to a large mound of earth they were led. As he came near to the mound, Swift Lance saw that it covered a cavelike room, entered through a gate fashioned of stout mesquite logs. Four frog people picked up the gate and moved it aside. Others freed the boys, and they were shoved into the cave. The gate was then shut. They stood near it, seeing nothing at first but blackness.

Gradually their eyes became accustomed to the lesser light of the cave. They saw other forms about them. Soon they could recognize other humans, men like themselves, who sat or lay about the cave. Old men were these, bent and dirty.

One came to them and asked, "Who are you? What is your tribe?"

Swift Lance recognized the tongue to be Navaho, but when he answered in Mohave, he saw that he was understood.

"Mohave hunters are we. Whence came you and your companions?"

"We are of many tribes," the old man answered. "Be not surprised that we have learned each other's language. There is little enough to fill the mind and keep it from madness." The tale of his capture was similar to that of Swift Lance and Shy Owl.

"You do not recognize me now, yet once when the tribes came together we raced to test each other's speed." He smiled feebly to see the amazement of Swift Lance. "Here too are other runners you will remember, runners most fleet of foot—Pima, Hopi, Zuñi, Apache, Comanche, Paiute, and Crow. Here in this cave you meet all that is left of the swiftest of our peoples." He fell silent then.

"But why runners?" Shy Owl asked. "What good are we to them?"

"They race us against each other. Race horses are we for these weird ones." A fleeting tone of anger touched the words, then it was lost in weary hopelessness.

"Then they must feed us well, as we see that our horses are sleek and well fed." Swift Lance was hungry, as he knew Shy Owl must also be; it had been long since they had eaten that rabbit in yesterday's twilight.

"Twice each day they bring us dried fish. Before racing they feed us swamp onions and other greens," one of the prisoners spoke up.

Even as they talked, their voices were swallowed in the croaking of many frog throats as the creatures gathered before the gate. Once again the hands of Swift Lance and Shy Owl were tied, and ropes were placed about their necks, that they might be led toward a small hill. The creatures followed. As they neared the hillock, the croaking died down. The beings waited.

Shy Owl was led forward first. His leader made him run up and down and forced his mouth open to examine his teeth. His legs were prodded and in-spected. Then the bidding started. Just as the sound had become deafening, one of the frog men stepped forward and claimed Shy Owl.

Swift Lance was sold just as quickly, to a neighbor whose mound was next to that of Shy Owl's owner. He was glad that they were close to each other and that the mounds were remote from the rest. Already he planned to escape.

Once inside the mound of his new owner, Swift Lance met the frog mother and her two daughters. He was given to the younger girl. She was dainty and seemed fond of him, sharing her food with him at once. When he had eaten his share of the dried bugs and grasshoppers, he was led to a corner where there were dry grass and leaves, his bed. He slept to the singsong croaking of the frog folk.

The next morning Swift Lance was led outside and tied to a post. A saddle and bridle were brought out of the mound. A bark pad was placed on his back, just below the shoulder blades. Over this the tiny saddle was tied. The bridle had no bit—only a muzzle, with a strap over the head, and reins. His small mistress was seated in the saddle, her webbed feet in the stirrups. His purchaser led him to a smooth and sandy race track along the shore. His training was about to begin.

Shy Owl was brought by his master. Other human

racers were led to the track, and every day they were put through their paces in preparation for the contest. Every day Swift Lance studied the mountains surrounding them, the lake, and its outlet. Every day as he returned from the track, he passed other humans, too weary and slow for racing now, harnessed to wooden plows in fields of mud. There worms and beetles were raised for food. Other humans dragged nets in the lake to catch the vast quantities of fish that must be dried and stored to feed the humans.

Swift Lance and Shy Owl, having come so recently, required more drilling than the other humans. Thus each day found them running longer on the track. Each day Swift Lance ran farther along the lake shore. One day he saw that a dam had been built to form the lake. He thought, "Without the lake, the frog creatures would be helpless. Their fields and food would dry up. They soon would die."

On the next day he paused to rest for a few moments near the dam. He saw a large log that seemed to be the one that held the other logs—it would be the one to work loose. He bided his time until a day when Shy Owl's master told him to run beside Swift Lance in a sort of trial race. As they jogged along, he shared his plan with Shy Owl.

"If I am able to loosen that huge log, the dam will weaken and fall. Those of us who can seize logs as they float free will be carried away on the surging waters before these frog beings realize what is happening. Tell every human you can. We must be ready."

"I will so do. How will we know the hour?"

"When the hour comes, we will know."

One by one the humans learned of the escape plan, even the old men in the big mound. They fed themselves hope with each mouthful of dried fish. Each grasshopper was enriched with the promise of freedom. As the time of racing drew near, the humans lived in a dream of rejoining their own peoples. Nothing was too hard to do, no work too wearisome.

The first day of the races dawned. Excitement was everywhere. The frog people bet wildly on the favorites. There were two days of drinking and dancing. Then came the peak day. The racers were led before the crowds, that their fine points might be admired. The fever of gambling possessed even the more conservative of the frog people. Even the old and decrepit humans were brought forth from the darkness of their mound to watch the races.

Guards were posted to watch over the humans, but gradually they were attracted to the side of the track where they could clearly view events. First, eight races were run. The winners of these races were to compete against each other. Both Swift Lance and Shy Owl ran in the final race, and Swift Lance won. His master was proud of his steed and gave him a bonus of dried fish before he took his family to join in the feasting.

The croaking cheering of the frog folk was loud as they moved to the largest mound, where a banquet was spread. Choice beetles, bugs, and worms were arranged in tempting display, inviting all to indulge their appetites to the utmost. In the frenzy of celebration, the frogs seemed to forget the captives.

This was the chance for which the humans had been long waiting. Swift Lance sent Shy Owl and two other humans to free the old ones from their corral. They were to gather the work humans and move in a body to the end of the race track and then to the lake outlet. There they found Swift Lance and others working to free the key log. Shy Owl dived into the water to help. The time was growing short—their captors could not gorge themselves forever. One by one the men on the bank slipped into the water.

At last the large log came free, letting the other logs surge to the surface of the lake. Each man clutched the log nearest him, and no human was injured in the turbulence. As the loosened waters roared away from the basin that had held them so long, they carried with them those who had been lost and long discouraged. Down the rocky valley and into a river the waters poured, and each man rode his log until he found a place that seemed familiar, a spot from which he could begin his walk home.

There was great rejoicing in the village of Swift Lance and Shy Owl when they made their way out of the brush and across the field. They could not tell often enough the story of their captors and the strange customs of that cursed land. Always there was one who had not yet heard the weird tale and would hear it from none other than him who had been there.

Years later they made their way again toward the north mountains and found that the lake had dried. Gone were the ugly ones with their threat for unwary travelers. The mountains had been freed of their curse.

THE FIRE GHOST

"My son, you are troubled?"

Falling Leaves' hand served bowls of steaming food as soon as Swift Lance returned from his day in the hills. He had gone to find the forage spots, the places where green feed was most plentiful, for there the wild things would gather as winter's cold drove them down into the foothills. Ever since his return he had said little; he seemed lost in his thoughts.

"It is nothing, Mother," he answered quietly.

Wise in his ways, she could see that he was not ready to talk of whatever had occurred. He went early to his night's rest, saying, "It has been a long day."

When he came for his morning meal wearing the same thoughtful expression, Falling Leaves was glad to hear him say, "I go this day to work in the garden of my grandmother." She knew the understanding they shared. The problem would be spoken as the boy worked beside White Flower.

Though the day was yet young, Swift Lance found his grandmother already pulling weeds in her garden. From her bending position she looked up to greet him.

"I have saved all the big weeds for your strong young back to fight," she said.

"That is good." Swift Lance took his place, pulling the largest weeds without further words.

"There is trouble in your voice, my son." Side by side they worked in silence through the rows of corn.

At the end of a row Swift Lance turned, still squatting, and began to talk.

"Many are the tales of our people you have told me, White Flower. Only one have you failed to finish— that of the chief who was lost forever. Something happened to bring you fright in the midst of your telling that night. You sent us all home. I had not again thought of that tale until yesterday."

The old woman straightened, stretching her muscles. "Let us seek the comfort of the willow where we have spent so many hours together."

When they had settled themselves at ease beneath their storytelling tree, she started to weave on her basket. "Now my ears are free to listen to the words of Swift Lance."

For a moment the boy waited. He felt more deeply about yesterday's experience than he had at first realized, and it was not easy to speak of intimate things, even to a trusted friend. He began to speak slowly but soon was so enwrapped in the telling that the words began to trip over themselves.

"As I returned from the hill pastures, it was good to be coming home to the warmth of food prepared by my mother's hands. My feet reached out, easily eating the distance. My mind was filled with pictures of young deer with their mothers and of the good things the hunt would yield for our people."

"You did not come to talk with me of the joys of the hunt," the old woman said, not pausing in her weaving.

After a few moments Swift Lance went on. "As I raced homeward, a small ball of fire, blue in color, rolled along beside me. It traveled not more than a long bow from me, yet I did not seem to notice it until it disappeared into the earth of the tribal cremation and burial grounds. When I lay upon my sleeping mat recalling the day's events, the blue fire came again to my mind, but I thrust it from me. When I slept, its ghostly glow lighted my dreams. What can you tell me of the ball of blue fire, White Flower?"

49

She stopped her work and spoke. "I recall the night you brought your friends to my lodge to hear the legend of an early chief who was lost forever, and I was frightened and sent you home. Let us talk of all these things.

"Many corn-planting moons ago the Mohaves had a mighty chief. He was called Red Hand. He was wise and kind, brave and strong—a good leader beloved of his people and held in respect by the neighboring tribes. There was none to dare question Chief Red Hand and ask why he always wore red wrappings about his hand. None had ever seen him without them. Now and again the chief went far into the hills of darkness to stay two or three days. Nor did any know why he went or what he did, yet he always came back wiser, with better ways for us to grow our crops.

"Once while he was away, a runner came from the leaders of the Warm Springs Apache Nation. They asked for help to make war on a northern tribe, the Paiutes. Since Red Hand was away, the second chief, Tall Tree, called a war council. Many young braves were sent to help the Apaches make war against the Paiutes.

"Only two days had the braves been gone when Red Hand returned from the dark hills. When they told him of the war party, the chief was angry, for he knew it was a trick to draw away most of the warriors, that the Mohave village might more easily be raided. Quickly he made ready to follow the Mohave braves.

"As he hurried along on their trail, he was ambushed by Paiutes. Red Hand backed against a huge boulder to fight for his life, hoping to give the village time to prepare for a raid.

"So it was that Red Hand fought mightily. At last he fell wounded so deeply that his attackers left him for dead and moved on to war with the waiting village. But Red Hand was able to gather his strength and crawl away slowly into his beloved hills. When the young warriors returned, they made search for his body. Every man in the village hunted far and wide, but they could follow his trail but a little way. At first there were those who saw Red Hand's fire ghost, but none dared follow where it led, and so at last it was seen no more.

"Mohave dead lie at rest only in the ancestral burial ground. No matter where or how a Mohave meets death, his spirit takes the shape of Wind Owl's fire, or lightning, and thus he roams the world until he is found or captured by his own relatives and brought safely home to rest forever.

"Now you say you have seen the ball of blue fire. Red Hand still searches for one who is brave enough to lead him to the burial place of his fathers. Else how shall he ever find peace with his people?"

Swift Lance was silent and thoughtful before he spoke. "I thank you, O Wise One. Let us pray that I may have courage, that I may not fail this charge. May I go with your blessing!"

And when White Flower had given him a grand-mother's blessing, Swift Lance hastened toward his home, singing the war song. His heart was light and his thoughts free of worry.

As he neared the burial grounds, the ball of fire sprang from the ground and rolled ahead of him. His scalp tingled, and his back was crawling goose-flesh. His legs were of a sudden weak, and he had to struggle with himself to keep from turning back to the comfort of his grandmother's dwelling. Reaching for his good-luck charm, which hung on a buckskin thong about his neck, he kept his feet moving in the path the fire ghost led. Fingering the rare and highly prized charm stone which had been found in the paunch of a newly slain deer, Swift Lance prayed for guidance, that he might help the wandering Chief Red Hand's spirit to find peace.

Through the darkness he stumbled, following the fire ball through rough terrain and ignoring the scratches of the brush that fought him. His flesh was bleeding where the stinging brush had whipped his face, arms, and legs. He ached with weariness, and a pain drilled into his side. The night was far spent, and the fire ghost seemed farther and farther from him.

Suddenly it disappeared into the greater darkness of a mountain.

With a final spurt of energy, Swift Lance reached the mountain and leaned against its wall until he could recapture his breath which had fled. While his lungs pumped new strength into his weary limbs, he looked about and saw a small opening in the mountainside. His hand gripped the bone handle of the knife he carried in his belt as he started headfirst into the opening, but he found the hole so small he would have to wriggle forward and so dark he could see nothing. He decided to await the dawn.

The fire ghost was impatient. All the rest of the night it went in and out of the opening or danced entreatingly about him. Swift Lance felt only friendly interest now; fear was gone.

As the first rays of the sun broke through the night, he was ready to leave behind the daze of exhaustion and re-enter the opening in the mountainside. The morning light went with him so that he could find his way from rock to rock along the ever-widening tunnel. At last he found himself in a cave with a smooth floor of white sand. His eyes were accustomed to the faint light, and there in the center of the cave he saw the dried-up body of a man, the left hand still encased in red buckskin. The many arrows protruding from the ancient body caused Swift Lance to wonder how Chief Red Hand could have made the journey to the mountain hideaway.

The bats that clung to the roof of the cave were not disturbed when Swift Lance spread a large buckskin on the sand and carefully placed the no-longer-heavy body of the chieftain upon it. Wrapping it securely, he placed the precious bundle upon his shoulder and began the climb out of the cave. Though his burden was not heavy, it was cumbersome in the narrow opening, and there were many slips and fresh starts before Swift Lance reached the sunlight.

The blue fire followed him to the very outskirts of the village, where he was sighted. A runner hurried to call the people to gather in greeting.

Weary, but glad that his mission was done, Swift Lance laid down the buckskin bundle before the village medicine man, who had led the people to meet him. Searching in the throng, his eyes met those of White Flower, and he made his way to her side.

"This is a proud moment, Son of my son," she said. "On the next day Red Hand will join his ancestors in the burial ground, and thanks to you, he will rest in peace."

Then did Swift Lance look behind him along the trail he had so recently traveled, and he said, "The blue fire ghost follows me no more."

COYOTEMAN

One day as Swift Lance came back from the hunt, he found almost everyone on the outskirts of the village. There seemed to be a state of big excitement. As he came to the people, he met his father, who told him that six young women of the village had disappeared while they were hoeing in the gardens. No one had seen them go; no trails could be found. There was great concern, for this made the third time young women had vanished. There was no war with any of the tribes. No raiding parties had come down from the Paiutes.

That night a council of war was held. Scouts were to be sent out the next day in different directions to hunt for signs. Swift Lance and Shy Owl decided to stay in the village.

The next day when some of the women went out to the gardens, Swift Lance went along, dressed as one of the women, while Shy Owl stayed back. Some time later Swift Lance noticed the women trying to brush off some dark dust that had gathered on their garments. As they did so, they seemed to fall into a trance, for they had sniffed some dust into their nostrils.

Swift Lance moved after the women as they started to walk single file following a large white coyote through thick brush, along twisting trails and finally to a very large boulder. Alongside the boulder was the thick foliage of willow. Through the willow shoots the coyote slipped, and the women followed. Swift Lance was last. As he pushed his way through, he was grabbed from behind. Green saliva dripped on his neck and back, and low growls and the snapping of large teeth fell on his ears. He was tied and thrown to the ground. He fell face up, and his heart skipped a beat at the sight that met his eyes.

There were many creatures, each of them the size of a large man. From the waist up each creature was coyote—large animal face, ears, and teeth, huge hairy chest, long arms, and hands with sharp claws. The lower half was human, with a breechclout around the waist, strong legs, and moccasins on the feet. They used a language unknown to Swift Lance. They carried no weapons, only buckskin rope and long whips. Swift Lance was strung up to a tree by his thumbs and left there for the night. All the women were led to a big hut.

He remembered then tales he had heard. One time while he and Shy Owl were on a trading visit to the Walapais, a runner from the Hopis told the story of a place high in the mountains to the west that was always hidden by smoke. No one had ever found a trail that would take him there, and any who chanced too near came away ill and could not talk again. It was said that long ago men who had been banished by their tribes had gathered together and formed their own village. They could grow no food. Only tobacco thrived in the soil, and it became their only food. As time went on, a change came over them. They became coyotemen.

Since they could no longer work the fields, they began stealing women from the different tribes. The coyotemen would spread tobacco dust over the fields where women worked. When the dust had taken effect, the white coyote, who long ago had been a man, led the women away to the secret village. The prisoners had no will to escape as long as they were sprinkled with the ashes of tobacco dust.

The next day the women of Swift Lance's village were led out to a field where they were put to work chopping down mesquite trees. Every day they chopped trees—dead, dried-up trees. These were then burned until there were only ashes. The ashes were then piled up; there were many such piles all over the fields. Finally the piles of ashes were spread out over the ground, and into the ashes tobacco seeds were thrown or planted. Tobacco grown in that manner was considered the best of all tobacco.

As the women worked, Swift Lance was kept tied up. They could not make him work, for the tobacco dust had no effect on him. He had managed to keep his rare charm-stone on a string around his neck. To whatever place Swift Lance traveled, there the people would try to make trade for the stone. Now, if only he could free his hands, he could rub the charm between his thumb and middle finger. He prayed to the storm clouds to come swiftly, for he needed the rain to further his plans for escape.

He had noticed that the coyotemen retired to a long hut for the night and did not come out until early the next day. If he could destroy all the tobacco, which was stored in a basket the size of a hut, the coyotemen would perish.

As the storm clouds came overhead and released the

rain over Swift Lance, his bonds of buckskin became
wet and loose, so that he was able to free his hands.
Then he rubbed his charm-stone. But as he did so, he
remembered that he had dropped his quiver that held
his bow and arrows and the poison for the arrows. He
had made the poison by pulverizing red ants, scor-
pions, and wild parsnips into a powder.

He soon reached the spot where he had dropped his
weapons, and after a search he located the quiver
among some bushes. He returned, freed the women
and led them to the trail. They became clear of head
because of the rain. Then Swift Lance sprinkled the
poison over the tobacco storage basket. He put heavy
logs against the hut where the coyotemen slept. He
then hurried after the women and led them until they
neared the village. At that time he went ahead and
gave the call of the horned owl. Soon he was met by
Shy Owl, who had been waiting to hear the hunting
call. There was great rejoicing at the arrival of the
party in the village.

Some days later Swift Lance and Shy Owl decided
to visit the smoke country of the weird people. They
found that the smoke no longer covered the secret
place, and the ashes had blown away with the wind.
The grass dwellings were destroyed, and there were
no signs of the coyotemen.

Swift Lance and Shy Owl made camp that night in a nearby spot to see whether any of the coyotemen came back.

Shy Owl spoke. "Do you say that your charm-stone that you wear around your neck helped you escape?"

"Yes, Shy Owl. There are many kinds of charms. Your own is a hunting charm, and without it you could never lead us to the best hunting grounds. There are fishing charms, dreaming charms, and planting charms. My own is to ward off evil or help in getting away from evil spirits who are half-people. When I was tied for two days to the tree, my thoughts for rain went from my charm to the spirit of the deer from whence it came. Then the deer spirit flew around until it found the clouds that carried rain and guided them to me."

The next morning they left for their village.

THE SPIRIT DEER

"Swift Lance, you are the last of the hunters to return to the village." Black Tobacco, the Mohave hunting chief, was concerned. "All the others came to my dwelling. Not one brought game. Not one reported seeing game."

"And the fishermen? Have they caught well this day?" Swift Lance asked.

"No fish have left the streams this day to fill the bellies of our people. We will meet in council and decide what must be done."

So it was that the men of the village came together before the dwelling of the chief. As they took their places about the council fire, the solemnity of the occasion deepened.

"Our storage baskets are nearly empty, and the long winter lies ahead," Black Tobacco said.

"There is no game to be found."

"The fish have gone to strange waters."

"Are the gods angry?"

In turn each brave spoke his thoughts. Swift Lance arose and waited recognition.

"Let us hear the words of Swift Lance. As he returned from the hunting grounds this day, he saw what may lead us to wisdom."

"Let Swift Lance speak," Black Tobacco said.

Swift Lance stood for a moment to collect words. "All day long we sought the deer, the bear, or other animals our people could use to hold hunger from our village. We found only old traces left behind by the animals when they deserted our hunting grounds many days ago. Our hearts were heavy, for we have only these short weeks of preparation for the long winter."

Every eye was fixed upon the young man.

"Thus it was that dusk drove us homeward empty-handed. Shy Owl and I, who had lagged behind the others in the hope that we might scare at least a rabbit from the brush, were silent in our sadness. We were nearing the first hills when we looked up, and there against the hillside stood a huge blue buck. His antlers were outlined against the sky. His eyes glowed red through the fading light of dusk. We could not move as we stared in surprise.

"Then he was gone. A strange current lifted the hair on our heads. Between us and the spot where the buck had stood, the twigs and leaves swirled as in a whirlwind. The rocks rattled as if beneath fleeing hoofs. Yet there was no wind.

"I dropped to my knee, pulling my charm-stone from its pouch. As I rubbed it, a wind sprang up suddenly before us. Sweat drops oozed from our foreheads. Many moments passed before we were able to make our way homeward."

He sat beside his father, having finished his tale.

Silently the men considered what they had heard. Unmoving, each stared into the fire. This was no ordinary thing. Perhaps the blue buck was a sign.

Black Tobacco stood and turned toward the shadows where the women lingered and listened.

"If White Flower is among us this night, she who has lived through more winters than any other of our people, let her step into the light of the council fire and share with us the wisdom of her years."

The old woman left her place of waiting and stood upon the chief's right hand. With her left hand clasping her forehead, eyes closed, she stood deep in thought. When she spoke, her right hand pointed toward the fire and her voice was quiet, yet it reached each straining ear.

"The spirit deer has come to tell us that one of his people died without reason. One of us has wasted a life. Had a rabbit been slain carelessly, the rabbit spirit would have brought the message to us. Until we find the one among us who did this wrong, there will be no game in our hunting grounds, for the ghost of the dying one has cried out to his fellow animals, and they will walk our hills and valleys no more."

White Flower folded her hands against her breast and opened her eyes. She turned and found her place among the women.

Black Tobacco spoke to the medicine man. "Has Leather Sack words to offer in our time of need?"

Standing in his place, the medicine man then told the people, "Since it is Swift Lance who has been favored by the spirit deer, let Swift Lance be chosen to seek him a second time, to follow where he may lead. Perhaps Swift Lance may discover the name of the wicked one, who has offended our little brothers of the animal clans."

And so it was decided.

Early the next morning Swift Lance left the village with his friend Shy Owl. They had not gone far when they came upon fresh deer tracks, and their hearts were glad, though their skins crawled with the strangeness of their mission. Deep into the hills they followed the tracks, to a valley that was new to them. Eyes watched from behind every tree.

Straight to the center of the valley the tracks led them, to a large flat rock. There they saw a crude drawing. A small deer writhed in the flames of a campfire. The suffering of the animal was so real that the young men reached forth to the rock, but at their touch it crumbled to dust. Having been given the answer their people sought, they hastened homeward.

The people of the village were gathered to meet them. As Swift Lance told of the burning fawn, a deep silence settled upon the people, and they waited. Only when Black Tobacco asked whether any knew how this terrible thing had happened did a woman step forward and await permission to speak.

"Even now my young son lies upon his sleeping mat, too sick to run with his playmates, and so has he lain since the day three weeks ago when he found a wee deer in a thicket and brought it to our dwelling. But the dogs caught the scent of the young thing and rushed toward the boy, barking fiercely. He was afraid, and in his fear he threw the deer into the campfire and watched it die. How may he make up for this wicked thing he has done?"

"Let us go to your dwelling and speak with the

boy," Black Tobacco replied.

The entire village followed Earth Flower, mother of the sick boy, to her dwelling, and the boy was brought forth to stand before the chief.

In words chosen with care, Black Tobacco explained to the boy how his act caused by fear had cost his people their winter's food, and when he saw that Iron Wood knew that their well-being depended upon his righting the wrong, the chief spoke even more slowly.

"This night when the fires are lighted, you shall walk beyond the last flickering flame to the edge of the hunting grounds. You will walk alone. When you reach the spot where you shall speak, you will cry out in a loud voice to the spirit deer. You will tell him that you are ashamed to have wasted the life of one of his people. You will promise never again to break any of the laws of the fields and the forest, of man and of animal. You will cry out with feeling, and if the spirit deer accepts your vow, our hunters will again find meat for the stewpots."

So it was that the animals came again to neighbor with the Mohaves, and there was no famine in the land.

THE COURTSHIP
OF SWIFT LANCE

The soft cool breeze coming from the mighty muddy river moved gently through the peaceful Mohave village, as if to keep from disturbing it. The breeze was blowing the night spirit blanket away, making it disappear once more into the dawn.

Only the ownerless dogs of the village were wandering around from dwelling to dwelling in their endless search for food. Then all at once the calm was shattered by the distant war cry of the Apaches. Mothers grabbed their children and what food they could reach and quickly fled to the prepared hiding places in the thick jungle of arrowweed growing along the river banks.

Warriors reached for their weapons and rushed

forth from their dwellings to gather at the big house where all important meetings and councils were held. From there they were sent to their places of defense.

Swift Lance upon hearing the war cry had gone to the dwelling of Shy Owl, from which they both went out beyond the village to scout. Soon they found an exhausted and slightly wounded Coyotero Apache runner hiding by a large mesquite tree. They helped him up and led him back to the village.

There they found the warriors ready for battle. First were the light-weaponed braves who would meet the enemy, armed with short lances. Behind them were the heavy-weaponed warriors, the older men who carried heavy mesquite war clubs.

Swift Lance spoke. "Go to the big house. We will come soon for a council."

Then Swift Lance and Shy Owl took the runner to the dwelling of Falling Leaves where they gave him food and tended to his wounds. Then they led him to the place of council where all were now gathered. Swift Lance stood before his people, holding his right hand high for silence.

"People of the Mohave Nation, a runner from the Coyotero Apaches has come among us. Let him speak first."

The runner rose. "I am called Klin-ne by my people. I have journeyed far to seek our brothers, the mighty desert warriors, the Amahbas [Mohaves]." He then gave to Swift Lance a red feather, the symbol of war. Then there was much talking and shouting by the warriors. Swift Lance again held his hand high.

"Let Klin-ne speak."

The runner again spoke. "War is being waged by the Coyoteros against the desert Pimas to the south. We ask our brothers, who are known as very brave even among the Kitanemuks, the Yokuts, the Alli-kliks, and the Chumaches who live beyond Tehach-api, their sacred mountain, the home of the sun. Many are the songs and legends of your people in battle, and now the great chief of the Coyoteros, Eskel-leshe-low, asks your help. There will be many horses to be taken from the Pimas. I have spoken." Then he sat down.

Swift Lance made answer. "We, as brothers, are bound to the Coyoteros by treaty to help in time of war. He who speaks for war will cross his weapon above his head. He who does not honor the treaty will lay his weapon behind him."

All the warriors quickly crossed their weapons above their heads and spoke as one, "Choose me, Swift Lance. I am ready."

Swift Lance chose but one hundred from among them, but these were the finest of the Mohave warriors. When the choosing had been done, Swift Lance spoke again.

"We will make ready now, for the journey will be long, and there may be danger."

The women then were coming forth from their hiding places, chanting low the war song of the Mohaves. Then they prepared the food the warriors were to take, gourds of ground wheat that could last for fifteen days and other gourds of fresh water.

Klin-ne then spoke. "We must travel the long way through the lands of the Walapais and Yavapais, who are friendly. On my journey here I came across three different groups of tracks made by Pima sandals on the short trail."

Then Swift Lance spoke to the warriors. "We will travel in four groups. Klin-ne will lead the first group; Shy Owl the second group; Ipa [Arrow], his brother, the third group; and I will follow with the last group. Every warrior will take with him some *ihore* [willow bark] to keep his mouth moist. But first I will visit Vahadha-mat-ha [Tobacco Wind], our wise Kwalhidhe [Doctor] who sees beyond the stars."

Swift Lance made his way to the Kwalhidhe's dwelling and found him waiting.

"O Wise One," Swift Lance spoke, "soon we depart for the land of the Coyoteros to wage war against the Pimas. What have you seen in the stars?"

The old man slowly raised his head. "Swift Lance, the mighty warrior, this early dawn I saw the death owl. That is a bad omen. There will be many deaths among our warriors. Wait three days until the moon is right."

"O Wise One, we cannot wait. Time is not too long for us to make the journey. We ask your blessings on us, for the battles will be long." Then he departed.

The group led by Klin-ne had left when Swift Lance came back, and the other groups were ready. The group of which Swift Lance was the leader had to wait until the sun was beginning to lose its warmth and the shadows were growing long.

Mohaves in their long journeys always move in a trot, which carries them rapidly, and before the spirit blanket of night had covered the land, they reached the first camping. Early the next morning the war party was on its way again. They were now nearing the land of the Walapais. The hills were higher, dotted with cedar trees and large clumps of squawberry bush, from which Masipa, the quail, would flush out in numerous coveys and scatter into the low, thick bear grass.

Parties went out to hunt Akwaka, the deer. Campfires could now be used for they were deep in Yavapai country. But travel was slow and hard in the rugged mountains, and at night the cold, thin air drove the Mohaves close to the fires. It was strange land to most of the men, who had never been in the tall pine country. On the fifth day they met some Coyotero scouts who had been sent to find them, and they were guided to the stronghold of the Coyoteros and on to the main village. Here they were greeted and given food and rest.

The next day Swift Lance and the other leaders held a war council with the Coyoteros. It was late in the afternoon when the council ended, and the leaders left the large wickiup and made their way to the outer circle of people watching the dance. Swift Lance was in the group that stopped directly facing the three chosen dancers, the most beautiful of the Apache maidens. The honored dancer was the daughter of the Apache chief, dressed in gray buckskin. To her right was the smallest of the three, a shy, pretty maiden in brown buckskin. To her left was a slim girl in white. Her sparkling dark eyes rested for a moment on Swift Lance, and his heart skipped a beat.

She had a small, even mouth, and her finely shaped nose matched her snapping eyes. Her long black hair was gathered at the nape of her neck with a buckskin string, then reached down below her waist. Three soft, small owl feathers tied to her bangs blew across her face in the mountain breeze, hiding her smile. Swift Lance kept his eyes on her, following her every move, never noticing when the crowd pushed him as they danced. Her piercing dark eyes seemed to bore through him and ask, "Why do you stare, stranger?"

Swift Lance turned to a young girl at his side and spoke to her. She answered shyly, "That dancer is called Moonbeam. She comes from where the sun is born each day, high in the mountains."

Swift Lance nodded and smiled, then pushed his way in among the singers right behind the three dancing maidens. He spoke Moonbeam's name softly. She turned partly around, which caused her to miss a step of the dance. The other girls were aware and giggled, and one whispered, "That tall Mohave is watching you." Moonbeam became angry, only to hide the warm feelings in her heart.

"I do not see any tall Mohave," she whispered back. Then she shyly turned around in a natural manner, glanced at Swift Lance, and with her eyes scolded him.

Swift Lance smiled. Then he moved out from the singers and went to the young girl.

"Will you tell Moonbeam that I will wait for her by the dead tree that has fallen into the river."

The girl smiled and danced her way close to Moonbeam and whispered to her the message. Moonbeam nodded, then glanced toward him. Her blazing eyes could almost melt Swift Lance. He took one last look at her before he moved away in the darkness. His heart was heavy as he neared the river. His thoughts asked whether she would come to him and answered him that she must.

Never before had his heart been warm for any girl. Now he could not think clearly. He wondered what he should do. What would Shy Owl say? He had not come here to find a wife.

On reaching the fallen log, he sat down, his thoughts divided between the coming battles, home, and Moonbeam. Suddenly he felt soft, warm hands close over his eyes. He reached back, seizing the arms, then feeling the buckskin fringes.

"Moonbeam!" he spoke softly. "You did come. My whole body feels warm now. I was afraid you had been spoken for."

She drew back, saying, "I have come because our leaders have ordered our people to make welcome the warriors of the Mohave Nation. You have sent for me. I am here. Is it that you are lonely for your woman in your faraway home? Why did you send for me? Who told you my name?"

Swift Lance stood up facing her. "In my dwelling there is only my mother. She and my grandmother have tried to find a woman for me, but my feelings have not been warm. Now, this day, I have seen you. Would it be against the laws of your people if I speak for you?"

"Are you not the leader of the Mohaves? It is the

custom of our people to those who are friends that they be so treated. I must go back to the dance. I will meet you here again the next night."

As she turned to go, she reached for his hand and raked her fingernails deeply across it. He felt his warm blood flow across his fingers and clasped her other hand across them.

She said, "I did that for all to see that you are spoken for." Then she whirled and was lost in the darkness.

Swift Lance felt proud of his scratches. Was he not a Mohave warrior? He felt like singing the Mohave bird song. The next day, after another council had been held and he had checked on his people, he again walked to the fallen log. He sat down and was deep in thought about the coming battles and Moonbeam when a small stone hit him between the shoulder blades. He pretended that it did not bother him and sat there, throwing pebbles into the water.

Just as a third stone hit him, he whirled about, to see Moonbeam in the act of throwing another stone. Her cheeks turned crimson, and a weak smile froze on her face as the stone dropped from her fingers.

He smiled. "You cannot hurt a Mohave with stones," he said, then held out his hand to her. Together they walked to the log, sitting down without a word. He reached into the cold running water and seized a handful of pebbles. Facing her, he gently tossed the pebbles at her until they were spent. Then she, too, reached into the stream, picked up a handful of pebbles, and gently tossed them at him until they were spent. She kept her head bowed but looked at him with upturned eyes.

"Moonbeam, I know this is the way an Apache brave declares his love for a maiden, and she for him. Among my people the boy braids the girl's hair, and she in turn braids his."

Moonbeam slowly untied her hair, and he braided it into two long strands. She then spoke. "I talked to my mother last night of you and my wish of going back to your country with you. No Apache brave has spoken for me. You must give to my mother what she asks of you or hunt the deer for one year. The other day four Paiute traders came to the village, and one wished to buy me. I hate Paiutes. They are eaters of grasshoppers and turtles. They started trouble and had to be chased away. I will be waiting for you when you come back from the battles." She turned and was gone.

That was the last night of dancing. There was a larger crowd, for other bands of Apaches had come from the mountains. Swift Lance took his place on the outside of the dancing circle and kept his eyes on Moonbeam. Suddenly two girls came up behind him and led him into the dancers. The face of Moonbeam was flushed, and the anger in her eyes flashed swifter than an arrow. She broke off from her dancing group, and sharp words were spoken between her and the two girls. She kept following, and Swift Lance knew that she was right behind him, for he felt a sharp pinch on his arm and then a scratch on his neck.

He broke away from the girls and stepped into the darkness. He was puzzled, for he had meant no harm. He went to the fallen log and tried to understand her anger.

Soft steps woke him from his thinking. He drew his knife and whirled around, flashing the knife in Moonbeam's face. With the anger that only an Apache may show, she spoke.

"Swift Lance, I will scratch your eyes out, then you may go to those two bad girls. You big ugly, you big bear. You can dance with all the girls in the village. I will go to the Paiutes. You Mohave fool!"

Swift Lance said, "A Mohave would not act like you."

She quickly replied, "I am not Mohave, I am Apache." She turned and was gone.

Swift Lance grabbed a limb on the tree and in his fury broke it off, falling into the water in doing so. He sat in the cold water, tossing what rocks he could find into the darkness. He got up and shook himself, dripping and cold, then he went back to the dance. He must find her and make her understand his love for her.

Moonbeam was nowhere in sight. He asked about her, but no one had seen her. So he went back to his dwelling. As he stepped inside, he saw all his belongings scattered about. He became angry and went back to the dance. But he was in no mood for it and once more made his way back to his dwelling.

As he neared the place he could see shafts of light through the arrowweed walls. He stepped in. A small fire gently burned in the center of the dwelling, a pot of stew simmered nearby, and his belongings were back in place. Who had done this, he wondered. Not Moonbeam; she was too angry. Perhaps it was the wife of one of the leaders. But he was glad, for he was tired and hungry.

He smiled as he ate. Then as he lay down on his mat, he felt a hard lump at his head. Lifting the bedding, he found a small buckskin bundle. He untied it and found a beautiful bead belt. He smiled, for he knew this was the belt Moonbeam had worn at the dance. He would wear it into battle in the coming days. Finally closing his eyes, he fell asleep.

THE FATE
OF MOONBEAM

Early the next day the Apache scouts went ahead with some of the Mohaves. Later the main body left, followed by the women and children. The young boys carried the weapons of the warriors, and the women spoke words of encouragement to their men. Swift Lance looked about him, but Moonbeam was nowhere in sight. His heart was heavy, and he wished to turn back and find her, but as leader he must go on.

Beyond the village the women and children stopped to watch as their loved ones went toward battle, some perhaps never to return. Early on the fourth morning the party came in sight of a Pima village of seven dwellings, where the scouts awaited them. A council was held. It was decided that a party of Yavapais and

Coyoteros were to attack that village while the others moved on to another village of twelve dwellings. A party of Apaches was sent to attack this village, while all the others proceeded to the main Pima settlement.

This village had more than one hundred dwellings and was in readiness, having help from the neighboring Maricopas. The first attack was made by the Mohaves under Swift Lance and Shy Owl, aided by the Apaches. The battle raged through the village; then the attacking force was driven out into the desert. Swift Lance led his warriors into a thicket of mesquite; small fires were built, and food was cooked and eaten. Swift Lance went among his warriors and found that ten were missing. Then he and Shy Owl went out to scout the village and make plans for the next day.

The next morning before the sun sent out his warm rays, the Apaches attacked the village, followed by the Mohaves. All day the battle raged; then with the help of the Papagos the Pima braves again drove the attackers out into the desert. Many of the Apaches had been slain, and they gave up, leaving the Mohaves to make their escape. In the running battle many of the Mohaves were killed or taken prisoner.

Swift Lance gathered together his warriors and counted but twenty who were able to fight and travel. So they took up the wounded and slowly made their way back along the trail of the Apaches. Even before they reached the Apache village, they heard the wailing and crying and the death chant of the women. Nor did Moonbeam meet them on the trail.

He told Shy Owl to see that the warriors were taken care of, and he made his way to the dwelling of Moonbeam. There he was greeted by her mother, who told him that Moonbeam had been captured by the Paiutes. She and another girl had followed on their trail, and they had been ambushed. The companion of Moonbeam had escaped.

Swift Lance then returned to his warriors and spoke to them: "I will go to seek Moonbeam. When I find her, I will take her home with me. Tell my people that I will be with them before the north wind chills the leaves from the willow trees. You are four days' journey from the village. There is yet danger from the Pimas; you must be on guard all of the way. Those of you who wish to leave now will be led by Shy Owl. Those who wish to stay and rest will be made welcome by the Coyoteros. You have fought well and bravely; now you may walk with honor among our people. You will be remembered at the council fires, and you will be told in stories."

Shy Owl then spoke. "Swift Lance, you and I have followed the trails of the deer, the mountain sheep, and the paths of the Forbidden Mountains. Yes, together we have traveled far to trade with other tribes. Many dangers we have faced, and always we have returned to our people. Now I ask that I may follow you. Blue Crane, the scout, can lead our warriors back. They have wives and children they have not seen for many days. We two can travel fast."

Swift Lance looked long at his faithful friend and replied with a smile, "Shy Owl, you have spoken wisely. Blue Crane will lead our warriors home. Travel swiftly now, my braves, to the land of your birth. Go before the Giver of Life falls behind the high mountains."

Then Swift Lance and Shy Owl began to follow the trail of the Paiutes. They had not gone far when Shy Owl stopped and pointed to a blackbuck bush. Swift Lance picked a buckskin fringe from the bush. There was blood on it. He felt that they must be leading her through the brush and cactus, but she was trying to leave a trail.

Swift Lance told Shy Owl that they should make camp, since the darkness was now slowly creeping all around them. When Shy Owl had built a small fire, he sat by his friend and watched the thin blue smoke spiral up to vanish in the gloom. Then Swift Lance poked the fire with a small stick, so that flickering flames darted in and out of the smoke.

"They may see the reflection of our fire and know

that they are being followed. Then they may decide to let Moonbeam go free," he told Shy Owl.

He murmured a prayer to each wisp of smoke and gleam of the fire, that it might somehow reach Moonbeam. Later, during the night, he suddenly stood up with a start as a chill went through him; yet there was no breeze. He felt that someone was near him and turned slowly, but only darkness greeted him. Then, from the stillness of the night, the faint call of the quail reached his ears. Or was he yet dreaming?

He remembered telling Moonbeam that he and Shy Owl used the call of the quail to warn each other when there was danger. He strained his ears, not daring to breathe lest the sound be lost. But it was a long time coming again, and now it was faint and fading away. Slowly he walked around the embers of the fire, but the only sounds were the hoot of the owl and the yelping of the coyote.

He could sleep no more, so he built up the fire into bright flames. On the far horizon the small gray shadows of the dawn were slowly rising ahead of the glow of the Giver of Life. A cold, sharp wind from the high mountains whistled through the pine trees, stirring life awake. He awakened Shy Owl, and they ate a cold breakfast of acorns and jerky and set out once more.

Soon Swift Lance found a broken arrow. "Shy

Owl," he said quietly, "this is a Southern Paiute arrow. We are on the right trail. But it could lead to Navaho country. They may wish to go there to trade her as barter."

Shy Owl answered, "It may be that they are trying to throw us off the trail. As soon as it becomes lighter, we will circle back and forth from this place. You go toward that slope, and I will scout the other direction."

Soon after they had separated, Swift Lance again heard the call of the quail. He waited, listening for the whistle to come again, that he might know whether it was that of the bird itself. But when the whistle came again, there was a little catch in the sound, so that he knew it was Shy Owl. He quickly answered and went in the direction of the call. He found his friend standing by a large boulder.

"This is where they made camp for the night," he told Swift Lance. "They tied Moonbeam at that spot. See the blood on the corner of the boulder? The ground is all scratched. She must have cut her bonds and hurt herself badly."

Swift Lance saw that it was so. From the signs he knew that she must have dragged herself out of sight during the night. Then Shy Owl pointed to further tracks.

"They were running when these tracks were made," Swift Lance said. "They know we are on their trail and have left her behind. Near here is a deep canyon— one trail leads to the bottom, the other leads up the slope. You follow the slope, and I will take the other trail." So saying, he was ready to go. But Shy Owl spoke.

"During the night I heard the owl call. I am not afraid for us, only for Moonbeam. I know you will find her, my brother Swift Lance, and if you do, I will wait until you have need of me." Then he placed his hand on Swift Lance's shoulder and turned away into the dawn. Swift Lance watched with pride as his friend left.

Then he made his way slowly through the brush and boulders leading into the canyon. At times he stopped to hear any call, but the only sound that reached his ears was the moan of the wind. Then he threw caution to the breeze and called her name.

From what seemed a far distance he heard an answering call that sounded like "Swift Lance." His heart stopped and the blood rushed from his head. He called again, and once more he was almost sure there was an answer, yet it might be only an echo or the wind playing among the boulders.

But suddenly the call came from above, then there was a cry as a form came hurtling down near him and landed among the rocks.

"Moonbeam!" he cried, as he rushed over and

gathered her broken body in his arms. He could feel her heart beating faintly, but with every labored breath life was fading from her once-sparkling eyes.

She looked up at him, and her eyes sent him a message.

"I have found you, mighty warrior of the Mohaves. Return now to the land of your people. I go now through the vigil where I will meet with the mighty one whose feet do not touch the ground."

Then her eyes gently closed, though a smile remained on her face.

Swift Lance laid her in the grave that Shy Owl had dug after he had slipped silently into the canyon. Swift Lance folded her arms across her breast and smoothed her long black hair.

Then he arose and raised his arms high toward the sun. "I leave you now, my fair Apache. I leave you to stay in your own land from which I would have taken you, Moonbeam, for that is what you are called. May you guide me back to my own land."

Then they covered the grave and placed large rocks upon it, after which Swift Lance placed his lance at the head of the grave.

Then Swift Lance and Shy Owl turned once more to the land of the Mohave.

BIBLIOGRAPHY

Peplow, Edward H. *History of Arizona*, 3 vols. New York, Lewis Historical Publications Company, Inc., 1958.

Kroeber, A. L. *Handbook of the Indians of California*. Smithsonian Institution, Bureau of American Ethnology *Bulletin 78*, 1925.

Spenser, Robert F., Jesse D. Jennings, et al. *The Native Americans*. New York, Harper & Row, 1965.

The CIVILIZATION OF THE AMERICAN INDIAN SERIES, of which *Tales from the Mohaves* is the 107th volume, was inaugurated in 1932 by the University of Oklahoma Press, and has as its purpose the reconstruction of American Indian civilization by presenting aboriginal, historical, and contemporary Indian life. The following list is complete as of the date of publication of this volume.

1. Alfred Barnaby Thomas (tr. and ed.). *Forgotten Frontiers:* A Study of the Spanish Indian Policy of Don Juan Bautista de Anza, Governor of New Mexico, 1777–1787.
2. Grant Foreman. *Indian Removal:* The Emigration of the Five Civilized Tribes of Indians.
3. John Joseph Mathews. *Wah'Kon-Tah:* The Osage and the White Man's Road
4. Grant Foreman. *Advancing the Frontier, 1830–1860.*
5. John H. Seger. *Early Days Among the Cheyenne and Arapahoe Indians.* Edited by Stanley Vestal. Out of print.
6. Angie Debo. *The Rise and Fall of the Choctaw Republic.*
7. Stanley Vestal. *New Sources of Indian History, 1850–1891:* A Miscellany. Out of print.
8. Grant Foreman. *The Five Civilized Tribes.*

9. Alfred Barnaby Thomas (tr. and ed.). *After Coronado:* Spanish Exploration Northeast of New Mexico, 1696–1727.
10. Frank G. Speck. *Naskapi:* The Savage Hunters of the Labrador Peninsula. Out of print.
11. Elaine Goodale Eastman. *Pratt:* The Red Man's Moses. Out of print.
12. Althea Bass. *Cherokee Messenger:* A Life of Samuel Austin Worcester.
13. Thomas Wildcat Alford. *Civilization.* As told to Florence Drake. Out of print.
14. Grant Foreman. *Indians and Pioneers:* The Story of the American Southwest Before 1830.
15. George E. Hyde. *Red Cloud's Folk:* A History of the Oglala Sioux Indians.
16. Grant Foreman. *Sequoyah.*
17. Morris L. Wardell. *A Political History of the Cherokee Nation, 1838–1907.* Out of print.
18. John Walton Caughey. *McGillivray of the Creeks.*
19. Edward Everett Dale and Gaston Litton. *Cherokee Cavaliers:* Forty Years of Cherokee History as Told in the Correspondence of the Ridge-Watie-Boudinot Family.
20. Ralph Henry Gabriel. *Elias Boudinot, Cherokee, and His America.* Out of print.
21. Karl N. Llewellyn and E. Adamson Hoebel. *The*

Cheyenne Way: Conflict and Case Law in Primitive Jurisprudence.

22. Angie Debo. *The Road to Disappearance.*
23. Oliver La Farge and others. *The Changing Indian.* Out of print.
24. Carolyn Thomas Foreman. *Indians Abroad.* Out of print.
25. John Adair. *The Navajo and Pueblo Silversmiths.*
26. Alice Marriott. *The Ten Grandmothers.*
27. Alice Marriott. *María:* The Potter of San Ildefonso.
28. Edward Everett Dale. *The Indians of the Southwest:* A Century of Development Under the United States. Out of print.
29. *Popul Vuh:* The Sacred Book of the Ancient Quiché Maya. English version by Delia Goetz and Sylvanus G. Morley from the translation of Adrián Recinos.
30. Walter Collins O'Kane. *Sun in the Sky.*
31. Stanley A. Stubbs. *Bird's-Eye View of the Pueblos.* Out of print.
32. Katharine C. Turner. *Red Men Calling on the Great White Father.*
33. Muriel H. Wright. *A Guide to the Indian Tribes of Oklahoma.*

34. Ernest Wallace and E. Adamson Hoebel. *The Comanches:* Lords of the South Plains.

35. Walter Collins O'Kane. *The Hopis:* Portrait of a Desert People.

36. Joseph Epes Brown (ed.). *The Sacred Pipe:* Black Elk's Account of the Seven Rites of the Oglala Sioux.

37. *The Annals of the Cakchiquels,* translated from the Cakchiquel Maya by Adrián Recinos and Delia Goetz, with *Title of the Lords of Totonicapán,* translated from the Quiché text into Spanish by Dionisio José Chonay, English version by Delia Goetz.

38. R. S. Cotterill. *The Southern Indians:* The Story of the Civilized Tribes Before Removal.

39. J. Eric S. Thompson. *The Rise and Fall of Maya Civilization.*

40. Robert Emmitt. *The Last War Trail:* The Utes and the Settlement of Colorado. Out of print.

41. Frank Gilbert Roe. *The Indian and the Horse.*

42. Francis Haines. *The Nez Percés:* Tribesmen of the Columbia Plateau. Out of print.

43. Ruth M. Underhill. *The Navajos.*

44. George Bird Grinnell. *The Fighting Cheyennes.*

45. George E. Hyde. *A Sioux Chronicle.*

46. Stanley Vestal. *Sitting Bull, Champion of the Sioux:* A Biography.

47. Edwin C. McReynolds. *The Seminoles*.

48. William T. Hagan. *The Sac and Fox Indians*.

49. John C. Ewers. *The Blackfeet:* Raiders on the Northwestern Plains.

50. Alfonso Caso. *The Aztecs:* People of the Sun. Translated by Lowell Dunham.

51. C. L. Sonnichsen. *The Mescalero Apaches*.

52. Keith A. Murray. *The Modocs and Their War*.

53. Victor Wolfgang von Hagen (ed.). *The Incas of Pedro de Cieza de León*. Translated by Harriet de Onis.

54. George E. Hyde. *Indians of the High Plains:* From the Prehistoric Period to the Coming of Europeans.

55. *George Catlin:* Episodes from "Life Among the Indians" and "Last Rambles." Edited by Marvin C. Ross.

56. J. Eric S. Thompson. *Maya Hieroglyphic Writing:* An Introduction.

57. George E. Hyde. *Spotted Tail's Folk:* A History of the Brulé Sioux.

58. James Larpenteur Long. *The Assiniboines:* From the Accounts of the Old Ones Told to First Boy (James Larpenteur Long). Edited and with an introduction by Michael Stephen Kennedy. Out of print.

59. Edwin Thompson Denig. *Five Indian Tribes of*

the Upper Missouri: Sioux, Arikaras, Assiniboines, Crees, Crows. Edited and with an introduction by John C. Ewers.

60. John Joseph Mathews. *The Osages:* Children of the Middle Waters.

61. Mary Elizabeth Young. *Redskins, Ruffleshirts, and Rednecks:* Indian Allotments in Alabama and Mississippi, 1830–1860.

62. J. Eric S. Thompson. *A Catalog of Maya Hieroglyphs.*

63. Mildred P. Mayhall. *The Kiowas.*

64. George E. Hyde. *Indians of the Woodlands:* From Prehistoric Times to 1725.

65. Grace Steele Woodward. *The Cherokees.*

66. Donald J. Berthrong. *The Southern Cheyennes.*

67. Miguel León-Portilla. *Aztec Thought and Culture:* A Study of the Ancient Nahuatl Mind. Translated by Jack Emory Davis.

68. T. D. Allen. *Navahos Have Five Fingers.*

69. Burr Cartwright Brundage. *Empire of the Inca.*

70. A. M. Gibson. *The Kickapoos:* Lords of the Middle Border.

71. Hamilton A. Tyler. *Pueblo Gods and Myths.*

72. Royal B. Hassrick. *The Sioux:* Life and Customs of a Warrior Society.

73. Franc Johnson Newcomb. *Hosteen Klah:* Navaho Medicine Man and Sand Painter.

74. Virginia Cole Trenholm and Maurine Carley. *The Shoshonis:* Sentinels of the Rockies.

75. Cohoe. *A Cheyenne Sketchbook.* Commentary by E. Adamson Hoebel and Karen Daniels Petersen.

76. Jack D. Forbes. *Warriors of the Colorado:* The Quechans and Their Neighbors.

77. Ralph L. Roys (tr. and ed.). *Ritual of the Bacabs.*

78. Lillian Estelle Fisher. *The Last Inca Revolt.*

79. Lilly de Jongh Osborne. *Indian Crafts of Guatemala and El Salvador.*

80. Robert H. Ruby and John A. Brown. *Half-Sun on the Columbia:* A Biography of Chief Moses.

81. Jack Frederick and Anna Gritts Kilpatrick (trs. and eds.). *The Shadow of Sequoyah:* Social Documents of the Cherokees.

82. Ella E. Clark. *Indian Legends from the Northern Rockies.*

83. William A. Brophy and Sophie D. Aberle, M.D. *The Indian:* America's Unfinished Business.

84. M. Inez Hilger with Margaret A. Mondloch. *Huenun Ñamku:* An Araucanian Indian of the Andes Remembers the Past. Preface by Margaret Mead.

85. Ronald Spores. *The Mixtec Kings and Their People.*

86. David H. Corkran. *The Creek Frontier.*

87. Ralph L. Roys (tr. and ed.). *The Book of Chilam Balam of Chumayel.*

88. Burr Cartwright Brundage. *Lords of Cuzco:* A History and Description of the Inca People in Their Final Days.

89. John C. Ewers. *Indian Life on the Upper Missouri.*

90. Max L. Moorhead. *The Apache Frontier: Jacobo Ugarte and Spanish-Indian Relations in Northern New Spain, 1769–1791.*

91. France Scholes and Ralph L. Roys. *The Maya Chontal Indians of Acalan-Tixchel.*

92. Miguel León-Portilla. *Pre-Columbian Literatures of Mexico.* Translated by Grace Lobanov and the author.

93. Grace Steele Woodward. *Pocahontas.*

94. Gottfried Hotz. *Eighteenth-Century Skin Paintings.* Translated by Johannes Malthaner.

95. Virgil J. Vogel. *American Indian Medicine.*

96. Bill Vaudrin. *Tanaina Tales from Alaska.* Introduction by Joan Broom Townsend.

97. Georgiana C. Nammack. *The Iroquois Land Frontier in the Colonial Period.*

98. Eugene R. Craine and Reginald C. Reindorp (trs. and eds.). *The Chronicles of Michoacán.*

99. J. Eric S. Thompson. *Maya History and Religion.*

100. Peter J. Powell. *Sweet Medicine.*

101. Karen Daniels Petersen. *Indians Unchained:* Plains Indian Art from Fort Marion.
102. Fray Diego Durán. *The Book of the Gods and Rites* and *The Ancient Calendar.* Translated and edited by Fernando Horcasitas and Doris Heyden. Foreword by Miguel León-Portilla.
103. Bert Anson. *The Miami Indians.*
104. Robert H. Ruby and John A. Brown. *The Spokane Indians:* Children of the Sun.
105. Virginia Cole Trenholm. *The Arapahoes, Our People.*
106. Angie Debo. *A History of the Indians of the United States.*
107. Herman Grey. *Tales from the Mohaves.* Foreword by Alice Marriott.